ALEXANDER FLEMING

Richard Tames

FRANKLIN WATTS
LONDON•SYDNEY

Contents

This edition 2003

Franklin Watts
96 Leonard Street
London
EC2A 4XD

Franklin Watts Australia
45-51 Huntley Street
Alexandria, NSW 2015

© Franklin Watts 1990, 2003

Series Editor: Hazel Poole
Editor: Dee Turner
Designer: Nick Cannan

A CIP catalogue record for this book is
available from the British Library.

ISBN 0 7496 5022 2

Printed in Belgium

From Scotland to London

When Alexander Fleming's portrait appeared on the cover of *Time* magazine, the subtitle to his name explained his importance in a single sentence: "His penicillin will save more lives than war can spend." Yet his great discovery was a result of sheer chance, just as it was chance that made him a medical researcher in the first place.

Alexander Fleming was born in 1881 at Lochfield, a farm outside Darvel, a small town in Ayrshire, Scotland. He was the third child of the second marriage of his father, Hugh Fleming, a farmer, and he grew up in a household with seven other brothers and sisters in all. The farm gave this large family a poor income but a healthy way of life. Young Alec, as he was known, spent hours rambling over hills and moors and became very knowledgeable about plants and wildlife generally. Throughout his life he was a keen gardener, as well as fit and healthy, with a love of sport and travel. As a boy he had to be fit — the walk to

Fleming's mother (above) **was born Grace Morton, daughter of a farmer. Lochfield** (below) **was his birthplace and home until he went to Kilmarnock.**

school in Darvel was 6 km (3½ miles) each way.

Alec Fleming liked school, despite the fact that a playground accident smashed the bridge of his nose and left him looking like a rather battered boxer for the rest of his life. At the age of twelve he went away to attend the Academy at Kilmarnock, an industrial town, where he boarded during the week with a relative. At fourteen he was sent to London to live with his half-brother, Tom, who had qualified as a doctor.

Alec completed his education at Regent Street Polytechnic, London, where he took classes in bookkeeping to prepare him for a career in an office.

In 1897, Alec Fleming started work in the office of a City of London shipping company, the famous America Line. The jobs given to him were routine and rather dull for a bright lad. The outbreak of the Boer War between Britain and Dutch settlers in South Africa in 1899 added a new field of interest. There was a call for young men to serve as part-time soldiers and so Alec enrolled with the London Scottish Rifle Volunteers. In the course of his training he discovered that he was a very good rifle-shot. Years later this unexpected talent was to play a decisive part in changing the direction of his life.

The South African war ended in 1902 without Alec ever being called to active service. But he decided to stay on with the London Scottish. Apart from the chance to go on taking part in rifle-shooting competitions, it also gave him the opportunity to play water-polo and to mix with other young Scots who, like him, were living far from their native land.

In 1901 an uncle of Fleming's died, leaving him £250 in his will. Suddenly he had a chance to start a whole new life. He could give up his boring office job and follow in the footsteps of his half-brother, Tom. He would become a doctor. Alec Fleming did not, at that stage, have the basic qualifications for entering medical school. But he had never found studying difficult and had an excellent memory. He learned Latin in a few months and, when he took the qualifying diploma, passed equal top of all the candidates. It was a performance of effortless excellence, which he was to repeat throughout his career. He could now choose which of London University's twelve medical schools he wished to attend. He had once played water-polo against St Mary's Hospital, Paddington. So to St Mary's he went.

St Mary's Hospital, Paddington

St Mary's Hospital was established in 1845 and, when Fleming attended it, was the newest of the London teaching hospitals. It stands in Praed Street, near Paddington Station, London's main railway terminal for the west of England. The surrounding area was notorious for its poor housing and even poorer inhabitants. If Fleming ever needed a reminder of the need for medicine to relieve the sufferings of the poor, he got it on his daily walk to work. Today, a blue plaque on the wall marks the location of the laboratory where he was to make his major discoveries.

When it was built, St Mary's hospital was on the edge of the West End of London. Slums soon surrounded it.

Sir Almroth Wright

Almroth Wright, (1861–1947), was the son of an Irish father and a Swedish mother. He was also a brilliant research scientist who came to have an important influence on Fleming's career. A great bear of a man, he was outgoing and assertive, in strong contrast to Fleming, the quiet young Scot. As Chief Pathologist at the Army School of Medicine, Wright had become greatly concerned with the problem of **immunizing** soldiers against infectious diseases. In 1898 he urged the War Office to have every soldier **vaccinated** before sending them overseas. The War Office decided to allow soldiers to volunteer for vaccination, but not to make it compulsory. That wasn't enough for Wright, who resigned in protest. In 1902 he joined the **Inoculation** Department at St Mary's and began to gather around him a team of outstandingly able young researchers.

Sir Almroth Wright wrote over 130 scientific papers in the course of his long scientific career.

From Student to Soldier

At twenty, Fleming was two years older than most of his classmates but he fitted in easily enough. A gifted student who learned easily, he had time to spare for sport and amateur dramatics. Even though he appeared to be taking his studies in a leisurely way, he was regularly top of his class and in his first year won prizes for both chemistry and biology. Later he won the Senior Anatomy Prize.

In 1904, Fleming passed the first part of his qualifying examinations. His studies now shifted their focus from theory to practice. In 1905 he took the first examination for the Royal College of Surgeons and in 1906 took his finals to qualify as a doctor. At that point he was faced with a proposal from John Freeman, a member of Almroth Wright's research team. Freeman was very eager to keep Fleming at St Mary's because he valued him as a member of the rifle-team. He also knew that there was a research assistant's job going in Wright's department. He suggested to Fleming that if he got the job it would enable him to pay the expenses of studying for further medical qualifications. Fleming thought it was a good idea, applied for the post, was appointed, and joined Wright's department. He was to stay there 50 years and to succeed Wright himself as its head.

As a member of Wright's research team, "Little Flem", as he was called, seemed hard-working but shy. He was, however, soon valued for his great skill in making laboratory equipment, such as fine-stemmed glass tubes, which had to be individually blown and shaped by hand. Fleming also gained a reputation for having a very cluttered and untidy workbench!

Much of Fleming's work involved taking swabs, or samples of human fluids, such as blood or saliva, and putting them in Petri dishes — round, flat glass containers with a lid — where they could be left for **bacteria** to develop. These bacterial **cultures** could then be tested and observed, making it possible to identify the bacteria causing a particular infection and to develop a suitable vaccine to fight it.

Fleming sat for his advanced examinations in 1908 and was awarded the University of London's Gold Medal for his outstanding performance. The following year he took the second part of the Royal College of Surgeons examinations and passed these brilliantly as well. He could now practise as a fully-qualified surgeon, as he had once set his sights on doing. But now he decided not to. **Bacteriology**, which he had taken up as a temporary job, was now to be his full-time career. And it had begun very promisingly. He had already started to publish articles about his research in medical journals. He had invented a new form of blood test for a particular infection. And, at

Almroth Wright's insistence, he had begun to take on his own private patients, whose fees helped to enlarge his modest income.

Even socially, Fleming was beginning to come out of his shell. Wright knew many of the celebrities of the day and often invited them to tea-parties at St Mary's, where Fleming could hear their views and conversation, even if he seldom joined in the chatter himself. George Bernard Shaw, the Irish writer, made Wright the model for the main character of his play *The Doctor's Dilemma*. Fleming himself was invited to join the Chelsea Arts Club by a grateful ex-patient. It was to give him a lifelong interest in paintings, but also gave him a place to relax and meet new friends outside the world of science and medicine. He even took up a peculiar form of painting of his own by growing different-coloured bacteria

A lecture at St Mary's. Fleming sits in the front row on the left-hand side of the gangway. Note the banked seats to give a clear view.

in Petri dishes so that they made a picture or a bold design, such as the Union Jack. By the spring of 1914, Fleming had such a busy life that, after thirteen years, he resigned from the London Scottish regiment. By the autumn he was back in uniform again. War had broken out between Britain and Germany. But Fleming was no longer a volunteer private in an infantry regiment. He was a lieutenant in the Royal Army Medical Corps.

Fleming's rapid promotion was chiefly due to Almroth Wright. Wright's personal experience of army medicine led him to volunteer his expert services as soon as World War I broke out in 1914. This time the army was willing to listen attentively to Wright's ideas and agreed to inoculate soldiers against typhoid fever, which had killed so many men in previous wars. As a result, deaths from typhoid were to be less than one per cent of what they had been in the South African war. Instead of the 120,000 deaths there might have been, only 1,200 were recorded.

But there were other urgent tasks to attend to. If losses from disease could be drastically cut down, battlefield casualties were still inevitable. Could anything be done

American Red Cross volunteers tend wounded at a casualty clearing station in France 1914. Devoted nursing, however, could not stop infections.

to reduce the numbers dying from infected wounds? Wright gathered his team of young bacteriologists around him, including Fleming, and set up a research laboratory in Boulogne, on the north coast of France, where the casino had been turned into a military hospital.

Wright and his assistants worked on the top floor, where there was neither a regular supply of water nor gas. It was only thanks to Fleming's ingenuity that they were able to work efficiently at all. For it was he who devised Bunsen burners which ran on alcohol, glass-blowers powered by fire bellows, and a system of borrowed petrol cans and pumps to supply water.

Fleming and his fellow workers took endless swabs from wounded soldiers to investigate the process of healing and infection. He soon showed that the soldiers' own uniforms, driven into their wounds by bullets or shell fragments, were a principle cause of infection. It was generally believed by army doctors that strong **antiseptics** were the best way to prevent wounds from becoming infected. Fleming demonstrated that this was not always so. In some large and complex wounds the antiseptic sometimes failed to penetrate all the cavities and crevices deeply enough. And some antiseptics could actually damage the body's natural way of healing itself, while failing to kill off harmful bacteria. Most surgeons found Fleming's argument difficult to accept and disregarded it, calling instead for even stronger antiseptics.

Little could be done, therefore, for many of the wounded. Fleming and his colleagues remained deeply distressed that they could not do more to relieve the pain and suffering they saw around them.

A Bunsen burner (below), **one of the basic tools of the investigative scientist, providing a simple source of controllable heat.** (Overleaf) **The young Fleming at his workbench — clutter was characteristic of his normal working style.**

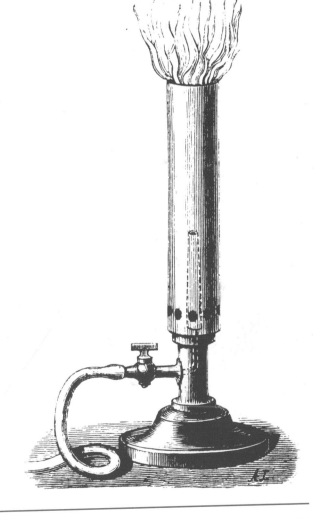

A Chance Discovery

In 1921, Fleming was appointed Assistant Director of the newly renamed Department of Pathology and Research at St Mary's Hospital. He was also given his own brand-new laboratory. It was there that he was about to make his first great discovery. But he could not know this. For the discovery was to be made entirely by accident — as a result of a common cold.

Over 50 years after the event, a junior colleague of Fleming's, Dr Allison, described how it came about:

" ... Fleming began to tease me about my excessive tidiness in the laboratory. At the end of each day's work I ... discarded tubes and culture plates for which I had no further use. He ... kept his cultures ... for two or three weeks until his bench was overcrowded with 40 or 50 cultures. He would then discard them, first of all looking at them individually to see whether anything interesting or unusual had developed ... the sequel was to prove how right he was ...

"Discarding his cultures one evening, he examined one for some time, showed it to me and said, 'This is interesting'. The plate was one on which he had cultured mucus from his nose some two weeks earlier, when suffering from a cold. The plate was covered with golden-yellow colonies of bacteria, obviously harmless contaminants deriving from the air or dust of the laboratory, or blown in through the window from the air in Praed Street. The remarkable feature of this plate was that near the blob of nasal mucus there were no bacteria; further away there was another zone in which the bacteria had grown but had become translucent, glassy and lifeless in appearance; beyond this again were the fully grown, typical opaque colonies. Obviously something had diffused from the nasal mucus to prevent the germs from growing near the mucus and beyond this zone to kill and dissolve bacteria already grown."

Fleming knew he had discovered something, but he wasn't quite sure what it was. He tested samples of

St Mary's in the 1960s — note the plaque marking Fleming's discovery.

The workbench where Fleming's great discovery was made.

nasal mucus from other people, to make sure that its bacteria-killing power wasn't just something peculiar to him. It wasn't. Then he tested other fluids, starting with tears, the one most closely related to nasal mucus, and going on to saliva, blood and even pus. He was surprised and excited to find that these very different natural products of the human body all produced the same result.

What Fleming had discovered was the body's own natural antiseptic, though it seemed it was not a very powerful one. Wright suggested that it should be called lysozyme, from the Greek word *lysis*, which means dissolving. Fleming gave an account of his findings in a lecture to the Medical Research Club. He was not a good lecturer and did not manage to convey the excitement or significance of his discovery. At the end of the lecture there were no questions from the audience, many of whom seem to have dismissed the discovery as interesting but trivial.

Undeterred, Fleming, assisted by Allison, carried on with his research on lysozyme. Even when he was supposedly taking it easy at The Dhoon, his country house in Suffolk, he would test garden plants and fish from the river to see how much lysozyme they contained. Fleming was himself convinced of the potential significance of his discovery for two reasons — it was part of the body's natural way of resisting infection; and it fulfilled the most important qualification for a bacteria-killer, because, unlike harsh chemical antiseptics, it killed off bacteria without damaging human cells.

Fleming discovered that lysozyme was 100 times stronger in egg white than in human tears. By injecting rabbits with egg white solution he demonstrated that their blood could be made more resistant to infection. Unfortunately, however, neither Fleming nor Allison had a sufficiently advanced knowledge of chemistry to enable them to make a pure form of lysozyme that could be used to treat humans. This was eventually achieved by researchers at Oxford University in 1937.

Today, more than half a century after Fleming's discovery, the importance of lysozyme is at last recognized. Uses have been found for it in preserving foodstuffs and treating eye infections. And the research into its properties and uses still goes on.

Fleming, in 1943, examining a culture in a Petri dish.

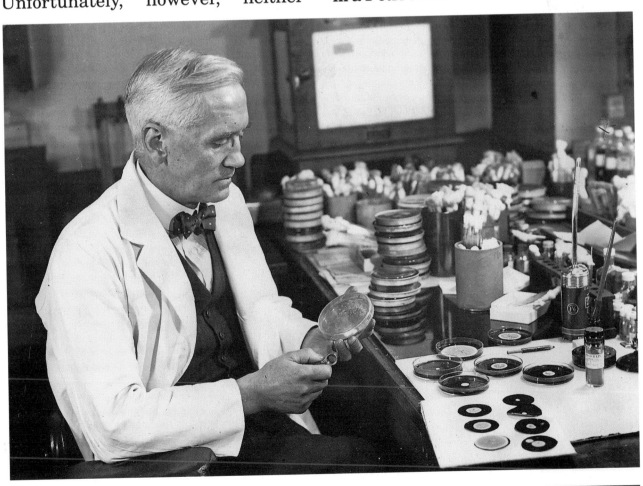

Howard Florey

A brilliant student and a fine sportsman, the Australian Howard Florey (1898–1968) graduated from Adelaide Medical School in 1921. He then won a Rhodes Scholarship which took him to Oxford and, later, via an exciting university expedition to the Arctic, on to research work and university jobs in Cambridge and Sheffield. As an editor of the *British Journal of Experimental Pathology*, Florey knew of Fleming's work on penicillin almost from its beginnings. He also had a long-standing interest in lysozyme.

It was Florey's initiative which got the Rockefeller Foundation in the United States to fund extensive tests on penicillin and it was his Oxford team which made it a treatment that could be produced on a commercial scale.

Florey worked tirelessly to develop the practical use of penicillin, flying to North Africa to work out its most efficient use on battle casualties and then to Russia to show the medical authorities there what it could do.

In his later life, Florey won many high honours. He became President of the Royal Society and Chancellor of the Australian National University, as well as being awarded the Order of Merit and made a **life peer**. He then became known as Lord Florey.

As President of the Royal Society, Florey attained an honour not given to Fleming — the highest British scientists can give to a fellow professional.

The Discovery of Penicillin

The way in which penicillin was discovered was remarkably similar to the chance manner in which lysozyme came to Fleming's notice, almost as though the one were a rehearsal for the other.

One day in September 1928, a former colleague of Fleming's, named Pryce, dropped in casually at St Mary's to see how the project he had been working on was progressing. Fleming, as usual, had an array of used Petri dishes scattered across his bench and was working his way through them before sending them off to be sterilized for re-use. He was at that time writing a chapter on the **staphylococci** group of bacteria for a new textbook and was therefore gathering examples of the ways in which different colonies of staphylococci varied from one another. Fleming picked up a couple of dishes to show the visitor, and then looked closely at one of them in surprise. The dish had contained a particularly harmful kind of bacteria, which normally grew into small, yellow-coloured colonies. But Fleming could see that a patch of mould had appeared on the dish and that around the mould there was a clear area, where the **germs** had apparently just disappeared. The mould, whatever it was, seemed to be able to kill off bacteria. But what was the mould?

Fleming set himself to investigate it systematically. He removed a section of the mould, put it in a separate dish and let it grow. Then he turned the mould into a liquid form and diluted it. Testing the dilute form on bacteria, Fleming found that even when it was only 1/500th of its original strength it would still stop the growth of bacteria. The mould was eventually identified as one of a group known as *penicillium*, named after the Latin word for a fine brush, whose shape the bacteria resembled. The particular variety that Fleming demonstrated to have bacteria-killing properties was *penicillium notatum*. Fleming decided to call his discovery "penicillin".

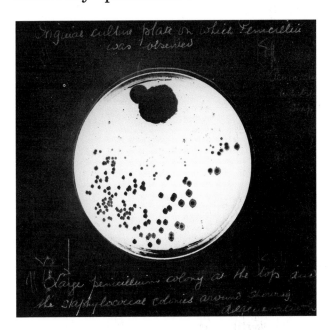

"Original culture plate on which penicillin was observed. Large penicillin colony at the top and the staphylococci colonies around showing degeneration."

As with lysozyme, Fleming next set himself to discover where else it could be found. He collected moulds from bits of food that had gone bad, from piles of rags, and even from old boots. None of them showed the anti-bacterial power of the original *penicillium notatum*. Meanwhile the penicillin itself was subjected to further tests to see whether, for instance, it produced undesirable side-effects. Fleming was relieved to discover that, while efficiently killing off bacteria, it did no damage to wounds or even to a surface as sensitive as the human eye. And the programme of tests also showed that, although penicillin was not effective against every kind of bacteria, it did work against many of the kinds that were most dangerous to human beings. Unfortunately, though, early trials on patients were inconclusive as it seemed particularly difficult to keep the penicillin active long enough for it to get to work fully.

Fleming's tests proved the potential of penicillin but did nothing to turn it into a useable drug that could be mass-produced for general use. He was, after all, a research bacteriologist and not a trained biochemist. He had done his job as far and as professionally as he knew how. He had made a strikingly original discovery. He had followed it as far as his expertise would take him. He had published the results of his researches so that others could learn from them. His article in the June 1929 issue of the *British Journal of Experimental Pathology* was the first-ever detailed report on what was to become known as an **antibiotic**. But at the time it aroused little interest.

A lecture Fleming gave at the Medical Research Club was met with the same indifference as had greeted his earlier address on lysozyme. Not surprisingly, Fleming turned his attention to other matters. His interest was taken by a new family of drugs, sulphonamides, for which many extravagant claims were being made. Fleming conducted a series of tests to show that while they could stop the spread of bacteria they could not kill them

Fleming's notes meticulously trace the life history of a mould culture experiment.

Ernst Chain, who cracked the problem of mass-producing penicillin.

off, a task which had to be left to the body's own defence mechanisms. Meanwhile, for almost a decade, the revolutionary potential of penicillin was ignored.

Hitler's rise to power in Germany led many German intellectuals to flee abroad. One of them was a biochemist called Ernst Chain, who chose to settle in England. In 1937 he accepted an invitation from Howard Florey to work in the Biochemical Department at Oxford University. Chain was interested in Fleming's 1929 article on penicillin and, with Florey's encouragement and the assistance of Dr N.G. Heatley, succeeded, where everyone else had failed, in finding how to make penicillin in large, pure, stable batches. This enabled extensive biological tests to be carried out by Florey and his team. One of their tests involved infecting 50 mice with streptococci bacteria. Half of the mice were then given additional injections of penicillin. After sixteen hours, 24 of the 25 that had received

penicillin were still alive. All the rest were dead. Other tests confirmed Fleming's ten-year-old findings and his claim that this dramatic new bacteria-killer was quite harmless to human beings.

In August 1940, a year after the outbreak of World War II, Florey, Chain and Heatley published an account of their research on "Penicillin as a Chemotherapeutic Agent", in Britain's leading medical journal, *The Lancet*. Fleming, who until then knew nothing of their work, read what they had done and came to visit them in Oxford "to see what you've been doing with my old penicillin." But he took no part in their researches and returned to his everyday work at St Mary's, tending patients in bomb-blitzed London.

Now that it had proved possible to make penicillin in a pure form, the next problem was to mass-produce it for general use. Britain was then deeply engaged in a war for its own survival, and desperately needed any new "wonder drug" to save wounded soldiers and civilians from dying of infected wounds. Unfortunately, however, the country could not afford to undertake a major programme of scientific development on a new discovery which had still not been definitely tried out on human subjects. So, in June 1941, Florey and Heatley decided to visit the United States in the hope of interesting one of the major drug companies in penicillin. Even if they could not find financial help they hoped to ensure that the secret passed into safe hands in the event of Britain falling to the Nazis. In fact their journey paid off handsomely when two laboratories agreed to produce batches for further testing in the United Kingdom. Even the United States government began to show an interest.

Over the course of the summer of 1942, Howard Florey's wife, Ethel, a qualified doctor, undertook a series of clinical tests of penicillin. She used the precious new treatment on a wide range of cases, from abscesses and surface wounds to deep internal infections. Her most spectacular success came with a two-month-old baby whose spine had been severely twisted by osteomyelitis, a severe bone infection. Six months of penicillin injections pulled him back from the brink of death and almost straightened out his spine. By September 1942, penicillin had been used successfully to treat 187 different cases. Ways had also been developed for using it in a variety of forms. In one form it was used as a solution to be swallowed or injected, either into the veins or directly into a muscle. In another, it was made into an ointment. It could also be added to dressings for wounds.

In the course of that summer, Fleming himself renewed his interest in penicillin. Florey sent him a sample to use in treating a case of **meningitis** afflicting one of his brother's employees. Within a few weeks the man was completely cured and discharged from hospital. *The Lancet* hailed the cure as definitive proof of the value of penicillin. It also called on the British government to find the resources to start mass-producing the drug at once. *The Times*, Britain's most influential newspaper, took up the cry and carried an enthusiastic leading article about this wonderful new discovery. It did

Penicillin immediately seized the public imagination. For once, talk of a "wonder drug" was scarcely exaggerated.

The fungus *Penicillium Notatum*, first source of penicillin, photographed many times its size.

not, however, inform its readers who had made the discovery. Almroth Wright soon set the record straight in a brief letter to the editor, stating simply that:

"Professor Alexander Fleming of this research laboratory ... is the discoverer of penicillin and was the author also of the original suggestion that this substance might prove to have important applications in medicine."

Following an approach by Fleming, Sir Andrew Duncan, the Minister of Supply, encouraged a number of British drug companies to begin to manufacture penicillin on a large scale. Soon it was used to treat casualties as far away as North Africa and the Pacific. By the end of 1943 it was sufficiently freely available to be used to treat factory accidents. And by **D-Day**, June 1944, Ethel Florey was in charge of a special penicillin unit in one of Britain's biggest hospitals. Here 3,000 rescued from the Normandy beaches were saved from developing gas gangrene, a most deadly battlefield infection.

Nobel Prizes

Alfred Nobel (1833–96) was a Swedish industrialist and the inventor of the explosives dynamite and blasting gelatine. He left most of his immense fortune to fund an annual award of prizes to the people who had done most of benefit to humanity in the fields of chemistry, physics, medicine, literature and peace. Awards are made on the recommendations of panels of learned Swedish experts and the winners go to Stockholm to receive a gold medal and a substantial sum of money. The winners agree to give a lecture, explaining the value and importance of their particular achievement. Prize winners for medicine have included Sir Ronald Ross, who discovered how to combat malaria, and Sir Frederick Banting, the Canadian discoverer of insulin, which is used in the treatment of diabetes. Fleming, Florey and Chain were jointly awarded the Nobel Prize for Medicine in 1945, for their work on penicillin.

Alfred Nobel, 1895 (below). **Fleming's medal** (below left) **bore a strikingly good likeness to the man himself.**

The Fleming Myth

Almroth Wright's uncomplicated claim that his junior colleague was the sole discoverer of penicillin began what Fleming himself delighted in calling "The Fleming Myth". A month after D-Day, in July 1944, King George VI knighted both Fleming and Florey. A year later they again stood together before another king, in Stockholm, where the Swedish monarch presented them, and Ernst Chain, with the Nobel Prize for Medicine.

Florey was a very private man. He refused to give the slightest encouragement to the press, who were eager to know what part he had played in developing what journalists loved to call a "miracle" cure. So it was left to Fleming alone to act as the centre of attention. His active research career was by now over, so he had the time and enjoyed the opportunity to speak out on behalf of science. But he was careful not to exaggerate what he had done, saying:

"Nature makes penicillin; I just found it."

Fleming, dressed in academic robes, receives yet another presentation gift, this time from the young Duke of Edinburgh.

And he always made it clear that it was Florey and his team who had turned it into a practical drug for doctors to use.

Nevertheless, the honours Fleming received reveal how it was his fame that spread across the world and won him a reputation as a saviour of all mankind. Britain, of course, was proud of him. He was made a **freeman** of Paddington, where he worked, of Chelsea, where he lived, and of Darvel, where he had been born. He was made a Fellow of the Royal Society and a Fellow of the Royal College of Physicians. The French made him a Commander of the Legion of Honour. The Pope awarded him a special medal. When he went to see a football match in Spain the entire crowd of 20,000 rose to their feet and applauded him. In the United States, Harvard University gave him an honorary degree and the Kiowa Indians made him an honorary chief of their tribe. In 1951 the students of Edinburgh University elected him as their **rector**. Dozens of cities throughout Europe named streets or squares in his honour. Even the British

Fleming in Athens with Amalia Voureka Coutsouris, a Greek medical researcher whom he married in 1953.

Fleming, chaired shoulder high by students at Edinburgh University, when installed as Rector in 1951.

Ministry of Health named one of its major office blocks Fleming House.

And Fleming, as tough and energetic as ever, enjoyed it all enormously. As a globe-trotting celebrity he travelled the length and breadth of Europe, visited the United States five times and was received with respect and gratitude as far away as Brazil and Pakistan. He lived a full and vigorous "retirement" until his sudden death from a heart attack in March 1955.

Summarizing Fleming's career, the British *Dictionary of National Biography* analyzed the qualities which made him a great scientist:

" ... an innate curiosity and perceptiveness regarding natural phenomena, insight into the heart of

Fleming and his second wife on their wedding day. After his death she returned to her native Greece until she was expelled for criticising the 1967 coup.

a problem, technical ingenuity, persistence in seeing the job through, and that physical and mental toughness which is essential to a top-class investigator."

Of Fleming the man, the author of this final tribute observed:

"He was sensitive and sympathetic, enjoyed the simple things in life and was not impressed with the grandiose. A collection of schoolchildren's signatures or a letter from a child or from some poor person who had benefited from penicillin gave him as much joy as the gold medals and honorary degrees … He was essentially a humble, simple man who to the end remained remarkably unspoiled and unchanged despite all the honours which were showered upon him."

By burying Fleming in St Paul's Cathedral, beside the greatest heroes and statesmen, Britain honoured him on behalf of many nations.

Drugs and Medicine

For thousands of years, people have known that some plants and other natural substances contained chemicals that could be used to treat illness. The traditional skills of the herbalist could often produce remarkable cures, even though nobody really understood why the cures worked. For example, quinine (a chemical found in the bark of a particular South American tree) was used to treat malaria. Digitalis (extracted from the foxglove) was used to treat heart disease.

The modern science of pharmacy (medicine-making) grew from the herbalist's art. The first anti-fever drugs and painkillers were discovered during the nineteenth century. Aspirin, still the world's most widely used drug, was invented in Germany in 1899.

Now that more is understood about chemistry and biology, the modern drugs industry produces a vast range of drugs to treat many kinds of illness. Some are extracted from plants; others are laboratory-made versions of natural chemicals.

A chemist's shop of the period when Fleming discovered penicillin, offering aids to health, beauty and pain relief.

Penicillin

Penicillin was the first antibiotic drug to be discovered. Antibiotics are chemicals, produced by micro-organisms, that can be used to destroy other micro-organisms, such as the bacteria that cause disease. Penicillin is almost completely harmless to the human body even if a dose 100 times greater than is necessary is given. However, some people are allergic to it. It can be taken in a variety of ways — by mouth (a usual method with babies) or more often by injection into a muscle. It can also be given as tablets, a cream (for burns), a pastille (for throat infections) or inhaled as a fine spray (for diseases of the lungs).

It was first used during World War II to treat battle casualties, and it saved tens of thousands of lives — and limbs. After the war it began to be used for civilians.

Penicillin can treat most forms of the killer diseases meningitis and pneumonia. It is also effective against anthrax, diphtheria, rat-bite fever and yaws. Blood-poisoning, once almost incurable, is now cured 90 per cent of the time by penicillin. It also destroys the bacteria that make wounds and sores turn septic. The discovery of penicillin led to the production of other kinds of antibiotics — drugs that have revolutionized medicine.

Culture flasks for the preparation of penicillin — the 1943 method of mass-production.

Find Out More ...

Important Dates

1881 8 August, born at Lochfield, near Darvel, Scotland
1895 Moves to London and attends Regent Street Polytechnic
1897 Becomes a clerk in a shipping office
1900 Joins London Scottish Rifle Volunteers
1901 Becomes a student at St Mary's Hospital Medical School
1908 Wins University of London Gold Medal
1909 Becomes a qualified surgeon
1914 Joins Royal Army Medical Corps as a lieutenant
1915 Marries Sarah (Sareen) McElroy
1920 Lecturer in bacteriology in St Mary's Medical School
1921 Assistant Director, Department of Pathology and Research, St Mary's

1922 Discovers lysozyme
1924 Birth of his son, Robert
1928 Discovers penicillin; becomes Professor of Bacteriology in the University of London
1940 Visits Florey and Chain at Oxford
1942 Cures meningitis using penicillin
1943 Fellow of the Royal Society
1944 Knighted
1945 Awarded Nobel Prize for Medicine with Florey and Chain
1946 Becomes head of the Wright-Fleming Institute of Microbiology
1949 Death of his first wife
1951 Elected Rector of Edinburgh University
1953 Marries Amalia Voureka Coutsouris
1955 Dies from heart attack

Useful Information

Alexander Fleming Laboratory Museum
St Mary's Hospital
Praed Street
London
W2 1NY
www.st-marys.org.uk/about/fleming_museum.htm

The Nobel Foundation
Box 5232, SE-102 45
Stockholm
Sweden
www.nobel.se/medicine

The Wellcome Trust
The Wellcome Building
183 Euston Road
London
NW1 2BE
www.wellcome.ac.uk

World Health Organization
Avenue Appia 20
1211 Geneva 27
Switzerland
www.who.int/en

Glossary

Antibiotic Substance that kills the bacteria that make people ill. Antibiotic medicines are used to treat many kinds of infectious diseases.

Antiseptics Chemicals that kill bacteria.

Bacteria Tiny one-celled life-forms that can be seen only through a microscope. Some cause rotting and disease.

Bacteriology The study of bacteria.

Cultures Experimentally grown bacteria, kept in special dishes so that their growth can be studied.

D-Day 6 June 1944, the first day of the British and Allied invasion of Europe during World War II.

Freeman An honorary title given by a town or city to someone who was born or lived there and who has become famous.

Germs A popular name for micro-organisms, particularly those that cause disease.

Immune Unable to catch a certain disease.

Immunizing Making people safe from catching a disease by first giving them a mild dose of it. The body then becomes defended against the disease.

Inoculation Another word for immunization, or immunizing.

Life peers Members of the House of Lords whose title are given to them as honours to hold during their lifetime only. The title can not be inherited by their descendants.

Meningitis A disease that causes swelling of the lining of the brain.

Rector The chief officer of a Scottish University, elected by the students.

Staphylococci Bacteria that cause pus to form.

Vaccines Substances used to immunize people or animals, making them unable to catch particular diseases.

Vaccinated Given a vaccine.

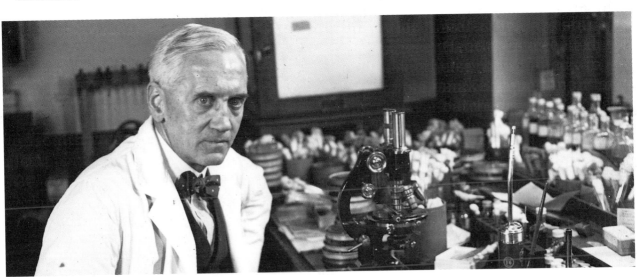

Index

Picture Acknowledgements

The publishers would like to thank the following for their kind permission to reproduce their photographs : Kilmarnock and Loudoon District Museum, 4 (bottom), 5,27; Mansell Collection, cover; Mary Evans, frontispiece, 6,10,11,22 (right); Museum of the Royal Pharmaceutical Society, 27; Popperfoto, 15,16,19,25,26,29,31; Science Photo Library, 21; St Mary's Hospital Medical School, 4 (top), 7,9,12,13,14,15,17,18,20,22 (left), 23,24.